TABLE OF CONTENTS

The 15 Point Road Restaurant, an eighty-seven-seat waterfront restaurant with the dining room overlooking the Sakonnet River, is located in the Island Park section of Portsmouth at, co-incidentally, 15 Point Road. The theme is one of casual elegance, where Classical music plays in the background and the wait staff, dressed in black and white, attend to each guest's needs. The restaurant has something special others do not, a pastry chef who also happens to be one of the owners.

The menu has many traditional American restaurant selections plus Signature Specials, which are interesting and innovative. The appetizer prices range from $2.75 to $7.95, entrée items from $11.25 to $20.00 and desserts $3.95 and $4.25. What's more, on Wednesday, Thursday and Sunday nights from October to May we offer, in addition to the menu items and specials, a Prix Fixe menu. The $16.00 per person price includes a glass of the house wine or draught beer, a house salad, a choice of one of up to 5 entrée items, dessert and coffee. There is a fine selection of wines available to compliment each meal and each guest's taste. We also feature a full bar which includes small batch bourbons and single malt scotches.

BREAST OF CHICKEN ELIZABETH

8 oz. boneless chicken breast, split
1 oz. proscuitto ham
Pinch chopped rosemary
1 tablespoon garlic butter
1 cup fresh spinach, packed
6 oz. basic brown sauce
1 oz. feta cheese
Salt and pepper to taste

1. Season the chicken breast with salt and pepper, lightly coat each with oil and place on a charcoal grill for about 4 minutes on each side.
2. In a sauté pan, sauté proscuitto and rosemary in 2 teaspoons of the garlic butter for 1 minute and add brown sauce, bring to simmer.
3. Using remaining garlic butter, sauté the spinach until it becomes slightly wilted.
4. Place wilted spinach on your plate and place chicken breasts on top.
Top chicken with sauce and sprinkle with small pieces of feta cheese.

Portsmouth, R.I.

15 POINT ROAD

© Muriel Barclay de Tolly 99

Liz Renshaw, the Owner/Pastry Chef/Hostess, began her food service career at Bailey's Beach. After a few seasons there, she went to Johnson and Wales College and earned a degree in Pastry Arts, graduating Summa Cum Laude. After graduation she worked at Cappuccino's in Newport and worked two seasons at the Breakers Hotel in Palm Beach, Florida. She worked back at Bailey's Beach as its Pastry Chef between 1990 and 1997.

Steve Renshaw, the Owner/Chef, began his food service career at the Pawtucket Country Club. After graduating from Johnson and Wales College with a degree in Culinary Arts, he began working as the Chef at Bailey's Beach. During the winter months he worked at numerous prestigious establishments in Florida. He worked as the Executive Chef at the White Horse Tavern in Newport, RI for two years and later returned to Bailey's Beach as General Manager for seven years. Just prior to the purchase of 15 Point Road he worked at Ocean Cliff in Newport, RI as the Food and Beverage Manager.

The 15 Point Restaurant is open for dinner on Wednesday and Thursday 5:00 to 9:00, Friday and Saturday 5:00 to 10:00 and Sunday 4:00 to 9:00.

15 POINT ROAD RESTAURANT

2

GUINNESS BEEF STEW

1 lg rump steak
2 tablespoons dripping
2 large brown onions, chopped
2 cloves garlic, crushed
1/4 cup plain flour
1 cup beef stock
1 cup Guinness
2 large carrots, sliced
2 bay leaves
1 sprig fresh thyme
Ground pepper
1/2 cup prunes, halved and pitted (optional, see Note)
Chopped parsley, for garnish

1. Remove any fat from the meat, cut into 1 cm cubes.
2. Heat 1 tablespoon of dripping in a pan and cook onions until pale golden. Add 1 clove garlic and cook 1 minute longer. Remove from pan and drain on absorbent paper.
3. Heat remaining dripping in a larger pan and add meat, cook quickly to brown on all sides. Reduce heat, stir in flour until all meat is coated. Blend through stock to form a thick, smooth sauce. Add Guinness and stir until mixture comes to simmering point.
4. Add onions and remaining garlic, carrots, herbs and pepper, stir until combined. Simmer gently for 11/2 hour, stirring occasionally to prevent catching. Cook uncovered so that sauce can reduce and thicken.
5. Served garnished with chopped parsley.
NOTE: If using prunes, add to pan in the final 30 minutes of cooking. The addition of prunes to this dish adds sweetness and balances the distinctive bitterness of Guinness.

Aidan's Pub and Eatery   1 Broadway   Newport, RI   02840   401.845.9311

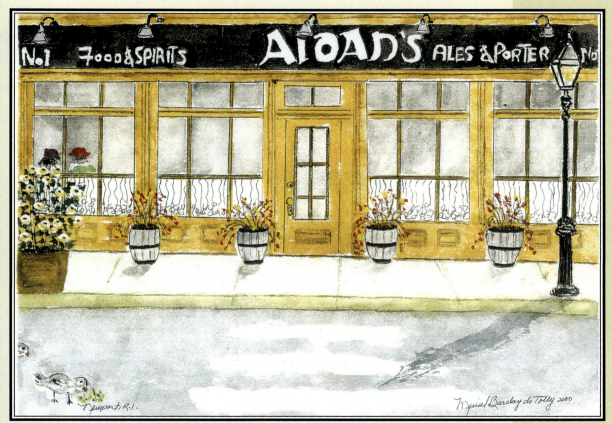

Aidan's of Newport is the only truly authentic Irish pub in town. It boasts a great atmosphere along with a large selection of draught beers and single malt scotches. Irish music sessions are featured on Wednesdays, Saturdays and Sundays and we offer a traditional Irish brunch on weekends. There are no strangers here, only friends that you haven't met yet.

AIDAN'S PUB AND EATERY

Bowtie Pasta with Chicken and Sun-Dried Tomato

1/3 cup olive oil
1/4 cup green onion, diced
4 tomatoes, diced
3 tablespoons freshly chopped garlic (or to taste)
1/4 cup sun-dried tomatoes, oil-packed
2 tablespoons fresh basil, chopped
1 teaspoon oregano
3 cups diced chicken (preferably barbecued)
1 lb. bowtie pasta

1. Boil pasta until cooked al dente. Drain, rinse and toss with 11/2 tablespoon olive oil and set aside.
2. Combine onion, garlic, tomatoes (sun-dried and fresh), and chicken and sauté in olive oil. Add pasta, oregano and basil.
3. Toss together and serve. Bon appetit!

Serves 4-6

April Cottage   John, Gail & Samuel Alofsin, Proprietors   Newport, RI

A mere mention of Newport brings warm images to mind... charming streets, mansions, Ocean Drive, beaches, the great salty air. When you stop to look at where we live it is so beautiful and breathtaking.

Our home in the "4th Ward", the "5th Ward" or "off Ocean Drive" (location opinions differ depending on whom you ask) is calm, peaceful and consistently smells like the ocean. Pockets of sunlight throughout the day and positive energy accent our home, so I offer a positive, healthy recipe for your enjoyment! Bon appetit!

APRIL COTTAGE

FILLET OF SOLE VANDERBILT

4 tablespoons garlic butter
8 fresh sole fillets
1/2 lb. bay scallops
1/4 lb. snow crabmeat
1/4 lb. mushroom, sliced and sautéed
1/2 lb. grated Monterey Jack cheese
1 cup hollandaise sauce
chopped parsley
Paprika

Preheat oven to 425°. Butter the bottom of and individual casserole dish with 1 tablespoon garlic butter. Place 1 sole fillet on the bottom of the dish and layer with a quarter of the scallops, a quarter of the crabmeat, a quarter of the mushrooms and a quarter of the cheese. Top with a second fillet and 2 tablespoons of hollandaise sauce. Repeat this procedure in 3 more casserole dishes. Place in oven and bake until the fish is flaky and the sauce bubbles, about 12 to 15 minutes. Top each portion with the remainder of the hollandaise sauce. Sprinkle lightly with parsley and paprika.

Serves 4

Brick Alley is a friendly, casual, professionally managed hot spot for lunch, dinner or cocktails. For over twenty years locals, tourists, and the Navy have made Brick Alley Newport's busiest year-round restaurant. Whether you want something fresh, cool, spicy, or sizzling hot, Brick Alley has just the menu to satisfy your appetite. Brick Alley also puts the "fun" in function at their new upstairs party facility, "Top of the Brick". All major credit cards are accepted.

BRICK ALLEY PUB AND RESTAURANT

SUNDAY AFTERNOON CHICKEN

When Muriel asked for a recipe, my instinct balked. I love to cook and consider myself an excellent cook but, follow a recipe... How do I write one, when I never use them myself? Anyway, there is a dish I cook that my friends and family seem to like from time to time. They say its kind of Southern, but only because all that I had in the "fridge" was some chicken and a jar of peanut butter. So here it goes....

1 package chicken thighs (any cut of chicken will do)
2 tablespoons each sea salt and coarse black pepper (I also suggest ginger and garlic)
~1 tablespoon olive or peanut oil
~1 cup extra chunky peanut butter

1. Prepare the chicken depending on which cut you choose. I find that cooking chicken with the skin on gives it a better flavor.
2. Coat the chicken with the sea salt and coarse pepper (or any other spices you like)
3. Add oil to a heated skillet (this dish may also be baked or broiled) and add chicken. Cook chicken on each side until cooked through.
4. When chicken is done, remove from skillet and transfer to an extra large crock or deep platter. Toss the hot chicken with the extra chunky peanut butter until melted. *Serve it without telling anybody what your secret ingredient is!*

Suggested Modifications:
1. Use pork instead of chicken.
2. Try flambéing chicken (or pork) when cooked through.

Broadway Florist Designs of Newport   210 Bellevue Avenue   Newport, RI   401.849.4000   800.637.7673

Newport, R.I.

Marie T Barclay diTally 2000

Broadway Florist Design Company has always been a maverick within the floral business in Newport; it has been a trendsetter without being predictably trendy. It is more than a florist; our designs have been featured in major national magazines, feature films, and have won numerous awards. Our forte is the daily challenge to design from the simplest to the outrageously decadent for both the particular and eclectic tastes of Newport. Broadway Florist Designs is a distinguished firm with a reputation for beautiful floral arrangements for the home, company, or private occasion. Please call on us to custom design your next floral request.

BROADWAY FLORIST DESIGNS OF NEWPORT

A PRIVATE AND CORPORATE FLORAL EVENT COMPANY

Maine Crab Cakes with Pepperonata Crème Fraîche

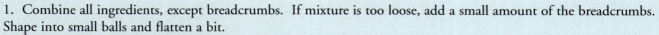

1 lb. Maine crabmeat
1/2 cup mayonnaise
1 tablespoon Dijon mustard
8 slices of white bread, crusts removed and bread diced in small cubes
1 shallot, finely diced
1 small red pepper, finely diced
1 tablespoon chopped parsley
11/2 cup breadcrumbs

1. Combine all ingredients, except breadcrumbs. If mixture is too loose, add a small amount of the breadcrumbs. Shape into small balls and flatten a bit.
2. Sauté cakes in vegetable oil until browned on both sides.

FOR PEPPERONATA CRÈME FRAÎCHE:

11/2 cup roasted peppers
1/2 cup sliced cherry peppers
1 cup crème fraîche

1. Purée both kinds of peppers in a blender and pour into a small saucepan. Add crème fraîche and bring to boil. If not smooth, return to blender.

TO SERVE:

Pour or ladle sauce onto a plate and place crab cakes on sauce and garnish.

YIELDS 10-12 CRAB CAKES (2 PER PERSON)

Café Zelda   528 Thames Street   Newport, RI   401.849.4002

Cafe Zelda, Newport, R.I.

Muriel Barclay de-Tolly 2000

The best little café between Bar Harbour and Key West is Cafe Zelda. If you are a traveler or a local looking for a favorite restaurant, this is the place.

CAFÉ ZELDA

Saucy's Strudel

FOR DOUGH

1/2 lb. butter
2 cups flour
1/2 cup sour cream

FOR FILLING

Cinnamon
Apricot jam
Chopped walnuts

1. Mix butter and flour, add sour cream and blend carefully.
2. On a floured surface, roll dough into a ball.
3. Wrap in wax paper and refrigerate overnight.
4. Divide refrigerated dough into four portions and roll each portion thin on a floured board.
5. Mix the filling ingredients together and spread on one portion of dough. Roll up and tuck in at ends. Repeat with other 3 portions.
6. Place rolled and filled dough on a greased cookie sheet and bake in a pre-heated 350° oven for 40-45 minutes.
7. Remove from oven and let cool slightly, sprinkle with powdered sugar and cut into slanted pieces.

Mike and Saucy Mureddu   Newport, RI

Newport, R.I.

Muriel Barclay de Tolly 2000

It was truly a happy moment in our lives when Saucy decided to take an engagement in Newport, Rhode Island during an America's Cup year. Mike, a native of Newport, met Saucy that year and the "native" married the "non-native". Our almost thirty years together has been a joyful and loving experience.

We are constantly mindful of how wonderful it is to live in this "City by the Sea". Historically, artistically, culturally, and musically, as well as in its beauty, Newport enriches our lives.

One of the first persons Saucy met when she came to Newport was Muriel, and they have been friends ever since. Muriel is a one-of-a-kind treasure with many talents. We are proud and honored to be a part of this exciting cookbook.

"Casa Del Canto"

If you seek Victorian charm, quiet solitude, great food and a "third" cup of coffee, then Chase Farm B&B and its warm, friendly hosts, Tom and Teresa Occhiuzzo, are for you. Their home is lovingly decorated with antique furniture from the Victorian era and collectible toys, dolls and games from the 1800's to the present. Bring along your grandma's favorite toy and Tom will be happy to give you an idea of what it may be worth!

Chase Farm Bed and Breakfast is located on two beautiful acres and offers a magnificent overview of the Newport Bridge, Jamestown, and the East Passage of Narragansett Bay. A panoramic water view and magnificent sunsets set the romantic atmosphere and highlight this lovely Victorian farmhouse just minutes away from Newport's attractions

Situated in the middle of Aquidneck Island, you are close to such attractions as Green Animals, Portsmouth Abbey, Prescott Farm, the beaches, St. George's School, Bristol, Fall River's discount outlets and Battleship Cove, just to name a few.

Chase Farm is also conveniently located next to the Newport Naval Base and Training Center and directly overlooks the legendary USS Saratoga and USS Forestall aircraft carriers, as well as the Battleship USS Iowa.

NONNA'S DOUGHBOYS

1 lb. pizza dough (from the dough setting of my dough machine or the local bakery)
~12 oz. good quality virgin olive oil
Powdered sugar or cinnamon sugar
You will need a good pot to fry the dough.

1. Let dough rise overnight.
2. Add enough oil to frying pot to fry dough, heat. To test cooking conditions take a pea-size section of dough and add to hot oil, it should rise to the top as soon as it hits the oil.
3. Cut off a small section of risen dough and pull and shape into a thin circle about half the size of your hand. Drop into oil and cook on each side until golden brown (do not burn!).
4. Remove to paper towel (this will soak up excess grease).
5. Repeat steps 3 and 4 until all dough is gone.
6. Place powdered sugar or cinnamon sugar in a plastic bag and add fried dough, shake to coat.
7. Eat and enjoy!

MAKES ABOUT 1 DOZEN

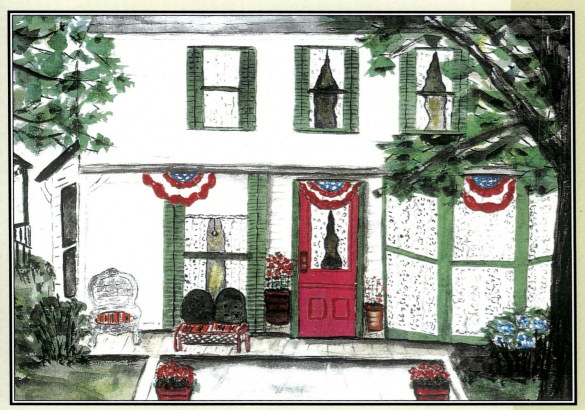

Teresa is a native of Newport. She inherited her passion to cook from her great-grandfather, an Italian immigrant named Anthony Razza. Anthony obtained his passage from Italy in the early 1900's to cook for the Italian artisans building the famous Gilded Age mansion, The Elms. Anthony passed on his love for cooking to his daughter, Columba, Teresa's grandmother. Following is one of Columba's (Nonna to her grandchildren) favorite treats that she cooked for the family on Sunday mornings. Teresa carries on this Sunday tradition at Chase Farm B&B.

CHASE FARM BED AND BREAKFAST

LEMON SNOW PUDDING

We used to beg our grandmother to make this dessert when we were visiting. I save it for the holidays as it is light and refreshing after a large meal and it reminds me of my grandmother and how much she loved to cook.

1 envelope Knox plain gelatin
1/4 cup cold water
1 cup boiling water
Juice of one lemon, strained
3/4 cup sugar
1 egg white

1. Soak gelatin in cold water for 5 minutes. Add boiling water and sugar and stir until the sugar is dissolved. Add strained lemon juice and chill mixture just until it begins to harden.
2. Beat egg white to a stiff froth and add to slightly hardened lemon mixture. Beat whole mixture until spongy. Chill until hard and serve with a thin custard sauce (recipe below).

CUSTARD SAUCE

1 egg yolk
1/4 cup sugar
1/2 teaspoon cornstarch
1 cup whole milk, scalded
1 teaspoon vanilla
1 pinch salt

1. Beat egg yolk, sugar, and cornstarch. Add scalded milk and heat mixture until it thickens, stirring continuously.
2. Add vanilla and salt and let cool. Serve with pudding.

Coffey's Texaco Station   Spring and Touro Streets   Newport, RI   Diane and Neill Coffey, Proprietors

Newport, R.I.

Muriel Barclay de Tolly 99

My husband and I were married in 1970 and a few years later had the opportunity to take over what had been George Gold's Esso gas station, located at the corner of Spring and Touro Streets. The interesting part of this particular area of town is that it is where the original town of Newport began. The town spring is located under a bronze plaque and located on our property, many tourists take note of it every year.

This lot of land has historically been known for transportation services, as it was initially where horses pulled up to drink and their owners caught the town comings and goings. As transportation became more sophisticated, so did the services that were required to meet the needs of a thriving community. Hopefully, we will continue to serve that purpose for many years to come.

COFFEY'S TEXACO STATION

We invite you to experience the luxury of the Francis Malbone House, an elegantly restored Colonial Mansion, circa 1760, conveniently located on Newport's Historic harbor front. Allow yourself to be pampered while enjoying our beautiful bedrooms, gracious sitting rooms and manicured gardens. Our personal attention to our guests and their needs is unparalleled in Newport. Our rates include a full gourmet breakfast, afternoon tea and off-street parking. Guestroom amenities include private baths (10 with Jacuzzis), fireplaces, air-conditioning, televisions, and CD players.

COLOSSAL COOKIES

1/2 cup softened butter
1 1/2 cup sugar
1 1/2 cup brown sugar
4 eggs
1 teaspoon vanilla
2 cups peanut butter
6 cup rolled oats
2 1/2 teaspoons baking soda
1 cup chocolate chips
1 cup raisins

Preheat oven to 350°. Cream together first 3 ingredients. Add the eggs. Mix all other ingredients in a large bowl and combine. Drop dough by rounded teaspoonfuls about 2 inches apart on ungreased cookie sheets. Bake 10-12 minutes or until set.

The Francis Malbone House

When visiting the 'City by the Sea' the only choice for luxury, value and first-class personal service is the Francis Malbone House, Newport's only Five Star Diamond Award-winning inn.

FRANCIS MALBONE HOUSE CIRCA 1760

Shrimp, Papaya, and Melon Salad

1 lb. large shrimp, pre-cooked and peeled (16-20 per pound)
1 honeydew melon, balled
1 ripe papaya, peeled, seeded and cut into 1/2-inch chunks

Combine melon and papaya and refrigerate until ready to serve.

DRESSING

1/2 cup red onion, chopped
1/4 cup fresh mint, chopped
1/4 jalapeno pepper, seeded and chopped (protect hands from pepper and keep away from eyes)
Juice of 2 limes
1 tablespoon balsamic vinegar
1 teaspoon honey

Combine ingredients and toss with fruit.

GARNISH

2 tablespoons fresh mint, chopped
Spinach leaves
Salt and freshly ground pepper to taste

Place decoratively on top of salad.

SERVES 4

Full Swing   474 Thames Street   Newport, RI   401.849.9494

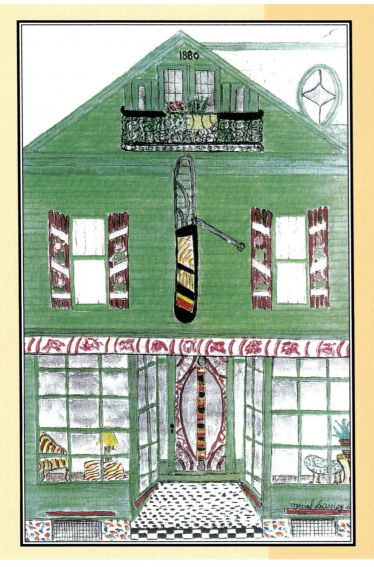

The building that houses Full Swing was built in 1880. From then right into the late 1970's this was known as the 'blue collar', 'meat and potatoes' part of Thames Street, not the tourist attraction it is today. Each of the store fronts around Full Swing were occupied by the butcher, the tailor, the plumber, the doctor, the grocer, the pharmacist, and the liquor store. In every instance, the family lived above their businesses and indeed it was a close-knit neighborhood.

FULL SWING

Veal Chops en Croûte

Freshly ground pepper
Kosher salt
1 cup white wine
1 cup water
5 garlic cloves, peeled and chopped
2 tablespoons finely chopped parsley
Olive oil
2 double cut veal chops, 12-14 oz. each
1 egg whipped with 1-tablespoon water
2 squares puff pastry
2 cups mashed potatoes
8 asparagus spears

1. Marinate chops in wine, water, garlic, salt and pepper for 2 hours.
2. Brush chops with olive oil and wood grill on high heat for 1-2 minutes on each side. Remove from grill and let cool.
3. Grill asparagus spears until tender.
4. Cut small slit in center of pastry square. Slide bone through slot and form pastry around chop. Trim excess pastry and seal. Brush with egg wash and bake in a preheated oven at 400° until golden brown, about 15 minutes. Let rest about 5 minutes.
5. To serve, mound mashed potatoes high on plate. Lean chop and asparagus on potatoes and garnish with parsley. Enjoy.

SERVES 2

GRAPPA   109 Long Wharf   Newport, RI   401.849.0011

....For your waterfront dining pleasure.

GRAPPA features a superb "made to order" menu of fine, contemporary, Italian-Mediterranean cuisine expertly prepared by our chefs and offered with the finest personalized service. Enjoy lunch or dinner inside or on the outdoor deck while enjoying a spectacular view of Newport Harbor. GRAPPA is open seven days a week and reservations are welcome.

GRAPPA

FRENCH-CANADIAN BREAKFAST CRÊPES

Unlike the dessert crêpes served in restaurants here in the States, French-Canadians prefer their crêpes in the morning. Also unlike us 'Americans' who like our crêpes stuffed with fruit and sweet preserves, French-Canadians choose to have their crêpes golden brown on both sides and topped with creamy butter and rich maple syrup. Sometimes they even sprinkle maple or brown sugar on them and roll them up.

2 fresh eggs
11/2 cup water
1 cup flour

1. Combine, but do not beat, the above ingredients.
2. Butter and heat a griddle until a droplet of water sizzles. Spoon batter onto hot griddle and allow the top to become dry.
3. Turn crêpe over and brown other side.
4. Enjoy!

Serve with thick slices of ham or bacon for a hearty morning meal!

Greenough Place   Newport, RI   Norman and Solange Langelier, Proprietors

1890s Cottage   Muriel Barclay deTolly 9

Greenough Place is a circa 1890's cottage, known as a 'working man's cottage'. It was one of the first of its kind in the Top of the Hill area of Newport and housed a community of summer residents, writers, and painters of that time. Our cottage has been restored to enhance its original beauty and continues to be a charming residence over one hundred years later.

GREENOUGH PLACE

PORTUGUESE KALE SOUP.... MY VERSION

3 lb. potatoes, peeled and cubed
11/2 lb. chourico (hot), cut into 1/2 to 3/4 slices
11/2 lb. stew meat
2-3 cans Progresso fava beans, drained and husked
1/2 head cabbage, chopped fine
2 carrots, peeled and cut into 1 inch lengths
1 extra large bunch of curly kale, separate leaves from stem
Salt to taste

1. Put stew meat in a large pot of boiling water about 1/4 full. Skim off foam. Add cabbage and fava beans (slightly mashed). Cook about 1/2 hour.
2. Add chourico, potatoes, carrots, and kale to simmering stew meat, cabbage and fava beans. Cook together for about 1/2 to 3/4 hour. Check potato to see if tender.
3. Salt to taste

Enjoy with a good loaf of crusty Portuguese bread and butter.

Harbor Antiques, Newport R.I.

Harbor Antiques not only offers antiques, but also painted furniture, and decorative accessories for the home and garden. A private, antique-furnished guest room is also available with parking in the heart of Newport. Open daily. Extended hours June through September.

HARBOR ANTIQUES, GOVERNOR SANFORD GUEST HOUSE

Swedish Meatballs

1 lb. round steak
1/4 lb. veal
1/4 lb. pork
1 egg, slightly beaten
1 cup milk
1/2 cup fine, dry breadcrumbs
2 tablespoons minced onion
3 tablespoons margarine
1 teaspoon salt
1/2 teaspoon pepper
2 tablespoons flour
3/4 cup light cream

1. Have butcher grind meats, or force through food chopper 3 or 4 times, using medium blade.
2. Combine egg, milk and bread crumbs; let stand for a few minutes.
3. Brown onion in 1 tablespoon of margarine.
4. Combine soaked crumbs, meat, salt and pepper. Mix with hand or spoon until smooth. Shape into 3-dozen balls about 1-inch in diameter.
5. Brown in remaining margarine. Pour off most of the fat, sprinkle meatballs with flour and shake pan. Add 1-cup hot water, cover and simmer for 35-40 minutes. Add cream and heat.
6. Serve meatballs with gravy.

1846

2000 JANE PICKENS THEATER 2000

Newport R.I.   Muriel Barclay de Tolly

"A Young Man's Dream that Came True"

Thirty-one years ago this May I purchased The Strand Theatre and renamed it the Jane Pickens Theatre. The Jane Pickens Theatre is the theatre I dreamed of for many years. Through good times and hard times, and with the help of many friends, I have succeeded in making my dream come true.

I would like to thank all my friends for all of the wonderful support they have given me throughout the years.

Joe

JANE PICKENS THEATRE

British-born Karol Richardson has been designing clothes since she was nine years old, whipping up exotic wardrobes for her sister's teddy bear. During her first year in art school she decided to take clothing seriously and transferred to the London College of Fashion.

Encouraged with having some of her first designs published in the London Sunday Times she set off for the United States and adventure. First arriving in San Francisco, her wild see-through jumpsuits caught the eye of a Los Angeles manufacturer where she worked for the next four years before moving to Manhattan and the downtown fashion scene.

Introduced to Wellfleet, Cape Cod by friends one summer, it was love at first sight. There was some serious soul searching before she decided to leave her Tribeca loft and head for the beautiful little seaside town with her daughter Natasha.

NATASHA'S PUTTANESCA SAUCE

When asked to include a recipe for Muriel's cookbook, I immediately thought of my favorite meal. It is one I've enjoyed, prepared numerous ways in many restaurants and homes. Muriel said it should be a 'real' recipe; this is most definitely that, as well as simple and always delightful. Serve this over penne with a gusty red wine and enjoy!

1/2 cup olive oil
1 jar (2 ounces) anchovy fillets, undrained
1 whole flower of garlic, crushed
1 cup kalamata olives, pitted and chopped
1/2 cup kalamata olives, pitted and whole
1 jar (2 ounces) capers, drained
1 large can (35 ounces) crushed tomatoes
1/2 cup chopped fresh Italian parsley
Coarsely ground black pepper to taste

1. Place the oil, anchovies, and garlic in a heavy medium-size saucepan. Mash thoroughly to form a paste and sauté.
2. Add 1 cup of chopped kalamata olive and sauté for 10 minutes.
3. Add the tomatoes, capers, and 1/2 cup whole, pitted olive. Stir and heat to simmering over medium heat. Reduce the heat to low, and simmer uncovered for 1 hour, stirring occasionally.
4. Add 1/2 cup chopped parsley. Stir into sauce and season with pepper.

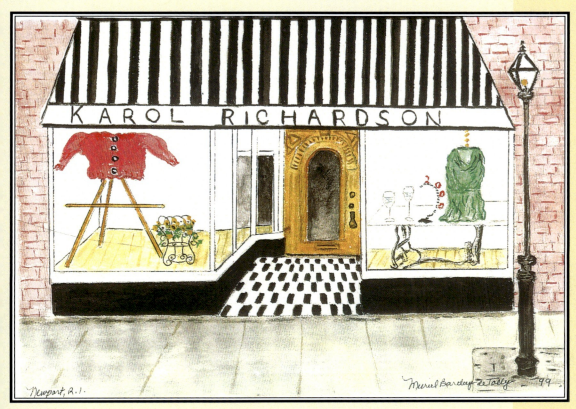

Newport, R.I.

Muriel Barclay de Tolly '99

When the shop in front of her building became available she jumped at the opportunity to show and sell her own designs, deciding to start small (literally) with children's clothes.

One thing led to another and children's clothes evolved into women's clothes. Karol now wholesales her line across the country under the Karol Richardson label. Her latest store, run by daughter Natasha, just opened in Newport, RI last year and has been a welcome addition to the town.

Recently Karol has designed costumes for a film that will be on screens later this year. She is particularly excited to have met an artisans group from Peru that will be helping her produce her new hand-knit sweaters and coats. Karol is also working on some very dramatic one-of-a-kind pieces for an artists benefit in Newport.

KAROL RICHARDSON DESIGN STUDIO

CROWLEY'S IRISH FILET MIGNON

1 8 oz center cut of beef tenderloin
2 slices Irish pork loin bacon

Remove all the 'silver skin' and fat from the tenderloin.
Wrap the steak with two slices of Irish pork loin bacon, use toothpicks or cotton cooking string to hold the bacon tightly to the meat. Leave the top and bottom (cut) ends uncovered.
Grill over an open flame to taste
Remove the picks or string and the bacon will stay with the meat

Newport, R.I.

Muriel Barclay-de Tolly 2000

The La Forge Casino Restaurant is located in the Newport Casino on fashionable Bellevue Avenue. The Casino was built in 1880 as a sporting club for the very rich whose mansions still line the Avenue today. In the summer during that time the Casino was alive with tennis matches, horse and flower shows, tea dances, and concerts. The La Forge featured a tearoom with fine pastries and handmade ice cream in addition to a formal dining room for luncheon and dinner.

While La Forge has changed with the times it has retained the atmosphere of the 'Sporting Life in the Gilded Age' and maintained its reputation for excellent food. The La Forge is now owned by the Crowley family who have brought to the restaurant an Irish flavor in Crowley's Casino Pub which serves stouts, ales and traditional Irish pub food.

LA FORGE CASINO RESTAURANT

Potato Omelette

1 large onion (preferably Vidalia), sliced
4 large potatoes, cut into small cubes
6 eggs
Cheese (any kind and as much as you prefer)
1 cup mushrooms, chopped
Salt and pepper to taste
2 tablespoons olive oil
1/2 cup milk

1. Par-boil potatoes until semi-soft.
2. Heat olive oil in fry pan and add onions. Sauté until golden brown.
3. Add par-boiled potatoes and sauté for 5 minutes. Add mushroom, salt and pepper. Sauté until mushrooms are soft.
4. In a bowl, whip eggs, milk and cheese and add to onion mixture. Cover and let simmer on low flame for a few minutes. Turn omelette when done on bottom.

Serves 4-6

Bellevue Avenue is home to the grand mansions of the wealthy. Coggeshall Avenue was the parallel street where staff lived.

When we were in the market for a home in 1991, this cottage was shown to us.

It had been built in the early 1900's by the chauffeur to Robert Goulet, the owner of Ochre Court.

It was rented and sold many times through the years, and progressed to a sad state of neglect and disrepair both inside and out. What had once been a lovely yard was now an ocean of weeds. But, in spite of all that, our first step inside this house convinced us that this was the house we wanted. (My friends asked why???)

The happy vibes from all her former tenants and owners fill this house, which we have lovingly restored to her former graciousness.

MAMMA P'S BED AND BREAKFAST

PORK IN PRUNE SAUCE

One 14-pound pork leg, cleaned and trimmed of fat
1/2 lb pitted prunes
Salt and pepper to taste
Vegetable oil for frying
1 quart Coca-cola
2 beers, bottled or canned
1 in. piece of Mexican cinnamon
2 tsp. piloncillo or dark brown sugar
5-6 cloves garlic
8 allspice berries
1 cup raisins

1. Preheat oven to 375°.
2. Using a knife, cover pork leg with slits deep enough to hold a prune and stuff with prunes, covering as much of the meat as possible.
3. Season meat well with salt and pepper.
4. Fry in hot vegetable oil in large heavy saucepan approximately 5 minutes per side. Transfer to cooking dish and add remaining ingredients.
5. Bake approximately 1 hour for each 2.2 pounds of meat (6 hours for this amount)
6. Remove meat and set-aside until cool enough to slice easily. Pour pan contents into blender and purée. Slice meat 1/4" thick and bathe in sauce.

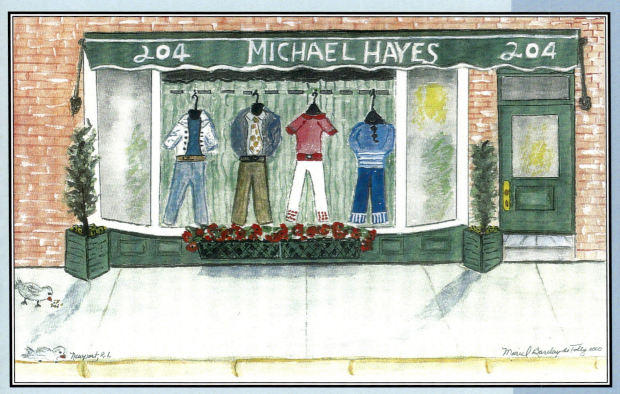

Michael Hayes, Newport offers a unique combination of men's, ladies and children's clothing; from ladies designer sportswear, dresses and resort wear to elegant hand-tailored men's clothing and casual wear and of course Michael Hayes fabulous kids clothes from France, Italy, and the U.S.A. Plus great toys too! Michael Hayes also offers on-sight tailoring and formal wear.

MICHAEL HAYES CLOTHING MEN WOMEN CHILDREN

CHICKEN BOMBAY/MURIEL'S RESTAURANT

This recipe remained the house favorite for many years.

31/2 lbs chicken strips	2 tablespoons curry (or to taste)
3 cups half and half	3 tablespoons flour
1/2 cup shredded cheddar cheese	3 tablespoons slivered almonds
1/4 cup raisins	3 cups cooked wild rice
1 large banana, thinly sliced	Salt and pepper to taste

1. Sauté chicken over medium heat in oil or butter, 3 minutes on each side. Set aside.
2. In a double boiler put half and half, cheddar cheese, raisins, banana, and curry and cook until very hot but not boiling. Add flour slowly, stirring constantly for about 10 minutes. This process will thicken the sauce.
3. Add chicken, salt and pepper (to taste) and lower heat. Cook another 10 minutes
4. On each plate, make a bird's nest with the rice and top with Chicken Bombay. Add a dusting of almonds and accompany with fresh vegetables such as broccoli or string beans
SERVES 4

ASPEN FRENCH TOAST/MURIEL'S B&B

3 cups corn flakes, finely crushed	1/3 teaspoon cinnamon
1/2 cup walnut, finely chopped	2 tablespoons brown sugar
6 eggs	2 tablespoons vanilla
	1 loaf of French bread, cut diagonally in thick slices

1. In a bowl, combine cornflakes and walnuts.
2. Beat eggs and add cinnamon, brown sugar, and vanilla. Mix well.
3. Dip bread slices in egg batter (soak well).
4. Coat soaked bread with cornflake and walnut mixture.
5. Cook in a well-heated pan with butter until both sides are well done.
Enjoy this winner of a dish with maple syrup, or fresh whipped cream and berries.

My last love affair with Muriel's Restaurant was painting this picture. I must say that after running Muriel's for several years, selling it was very painful. What I miss most are the wonderful people and friends who frequented my place. All of these watercolors have been a source of healing from that loss.

My new venture is my B&B which is very cozy and offers off-street parking, private bath and entranceway. 10 Pell Street is within walking distance to many, if not all, of the attractions in and around Newport. À Bientôt!

MURIEL'S RESTAURANT

Spanikopita or "Spinach Pies"

1 box filo dough
3 lbs. frozen chopped spinach
2 cups Parmesan cheese
2 cups crumbled feta cheese
4 eggs
1/4 cup chopped scallions

1. Preheat oven to 350°.
2. Mix spinach, eggs, Parmesan, scallions, and feta together.
3. Fold 3 sheets filo dough in 1/2 and place 6 oz. of spinach mix at one end. Fold over into a triangle and brush with melted butter or margarine. Repeat folding and brushing until you use all of the dough.
4. Repeat procedure for each pie.
5. Bake at 350° for 20 minutes or until golden brown.

YIELD 6-7 PIES

It takes something more than quick delivery and a thick crust to give durability to a pizzeria! We know, for we have been located at 38 Memorial Boulevard for nearly twenty years (plenty of free parking by the way). The key is a family atmosphere and a dedication to making each item we serve the best of it's kind. We use only top-shelf ingredients from imported meats to locally grown vegetables. But we think our customers will agree the secret is in the crust!

NIKOLAS PIZZA

Brisket Roasted with Red Wine, Leeks, Tomato and Peppercorns

1-5 lb. brisket or shoulder roast
1 to 2 tablespoons olive oil
2 tablespoons fresh rosemary, minced
2 tablespoons fresh thyme leaves
4 cloves garlic, minced
3 whole leeks, cleaned and cut into 1/2 inch rings
3 cups red wine
One 16 oz. can whole tomatoes
Whole thyme leaves

FOR BRISKET:
1. Preheat oven to 325°.
2. In a heavy pot or Dutch oven heat olive oil and sear the brisket until lightly browned on all sides. Remove meat from pan and let cool for several minutes.
3. In a small bowl combine rosemary, 2 tablespoons thyme and garlic. Rub the seared brisket with herb mixture. Place leeks in the bottom of the Dutch oven and place the brisket on top. Pour wine and tomatoes around brisket and sprinkle with peppercorns.
4. Bake, covered, for 3 hours, basting frequently. Make sure the meat is fork-tender when you remove it from the oven. Cool and place in refrigerator overnight and remove congealed fat from surface.

FOR SAUCE:
1. Remove meat and reduce liquid in Dutch oven by 1/2
2. Strain the liquid into a saucepan and heat to a simmer. Whisk in fresh thyme leaves and salt and pepper to taste.
3. Return brisket to sauce and reheat before serving. Serve over egg noodles or potato latkes.

SERVES 8

Papers is a full-service stationery store carrying small gifts and unique greeting cards, including those created by local artists.

Judith Carroll, a native Newporter, has owned Papers for four years. She and her knowledgeable staff are available seven days a week to answer all of your questions about printing and can even help you with social and wedding etiquette queries.

Whether you are looking for engraved wedding invitations or personalized stationery, come in and we will help you put your plans 'on paper'.

PAPERS

Native Seafood in Fra Diavolo with Rhode Island Lobsters

32 mussels, scrubbed and debearded
16 littlenecks, scrubbed
Twenty 20-30 size dry sea scallops
Eight U-12 size white shrimp, peeled and deveined
12 oz. white sea clams in juice, chopped
Four 11/4 lb. lobsters, boiled in water for seven minutes and put aside
One 28 oz. can Pastene tomatoes in juice, puréed in a food processor and set aside
1/2 each yellow, green and red pepper, large dice
1/2 yellow Spanish onion, small dice
4 oz. fresh garlic, chopped

4 oz. ladle shrimp stock (recipe follows)
Six A-size button mushrooms, sliced
2 oz. unsalted butter, rolled in flour
1 oz. olive oil
4 oz. bar brandy
2 lbs. linguine, cooked al dente and set aside
1 teaspoon each salt and pepper
1 teaspoon each basil, oregano and crushed red pepper
1 packet Spanish Goya spice

1. Place a large sauté pan over medium high heat and add olive oil. When heated add all peppers, Spanish onion and mushrooms. Next add littlenecks, mussels, scallops and garlic and continue stirring. When scallops and garlic begin to brown, deglaze the pan with the brandy (cook brandy down while stirring). After deglazing add remaining ingredients, except butter, and stir. Cover pan until mixture begins to boil, stirring occasionally. Add floured butter and cook until incorporated into sauce, about 2 minutes. When shellfish opens and shrimp become opaque, it is ready to serve.
2. Reboil pasta and place on a very large platter. Distribute Fra Diavolo over pasta and distribute shellfish around edge of platter.
3. Reboil lobsters until heated through and place in center of platter. It is optional to break open lobster and arrange on platter.

SHRIMP STOCK

Shrimp shells from 1-2 lbs. shrimp
1 oz. tomato paste
1/2 cup white wine
3 cups water
1 rib celery, small dice

1 carrot, small dice
1/4 onion, small dice
Salt and pepper to taste
1 tablespoon olive oil

Heat oil in small saucepan on medium high heat. Add shrimp shells with tomato paste, celery, carrot and onion and brown, stirring constantly. Cook 5-10 minutes. Deglaze browned mixture with wine and add water; bring to boil. Add salt and pepper and cook, let reduce to 1/2 and then strain stock into bain-marie.

Percy's Bistro   343 Lower Thames Street   Newport, RI   401.849.7895

Percy's Bistro. Newport, R.I.

Muriel Barclay de Tolly 2000

PERCY'S BISTRO

Percy's Bistro, the newest restaurant to open in the already hustling and bustling downtown area of Newport, Rhode Island, opened in May of 1998 in the landmark building of Salas' family restaurant. Percy's Bistro is located at 341-343 Lower Thames Street and is unique from the other bistros in Newport in that it is an American bistro serving American eclectic cuisine in a warm and casual atmosphere. Fresh seafood and pasta dishes are what dominate the menu. Percy Cook, the chef and concept owner has created and developed many different venues on Aquidneck Island and produces menus to incorporate current food trends throughout the country. In season, the Bistro is open for lunch and dinner seven days a week and is available for private parties for as many as sixty people. The Bistro is perfect for a wedding rehearsal dinner.

Chicken Portabella with Penne

2 1/2 lbs. chicken, diced
2 cups flour, seasoned with salt and pepper
1/2 cup olive oil
6 each portabella mushrooms, sliced
1 bunch scallion, diced
1 cup sun-dried tomatoes, soaked in warm water
5 cloves fresh garlic, diced fine
11/2 cup white wine

3 cups fresh chicken stock
1 stick butter, melted
3 tablespoons flour
1/2 bunch fresh parsley, chopped fine
1/2 cup grated Peccorino Romano cheese
Salt and pepper to taste
11/2 lb. penne pasta

1. Heat 1/2 oil in large sauté pan or saucepan.
2. Dredge chicken in seasoned flour and sauté in hot olive oil, when chicken looks cooked on the outside remove from pan and set aside.
3. Place remaining olive oil into same skillet and add portabella mushrooms, sauté for 2 minutes and then add scallions, garlic, and sun-dried tomatoes (cut julienne and reserve water). Let sauté for 3-4 minutes and add white wine. Let reduce and then add chicken stock. Bring to a simmer and add chicken and 3 ounces of reserved sun-dried tomato liquid. Bring to a very low simmer.
4. In a small saucepan melt stick of butter and add flour to make a soft roux. Cook very low for 1-2 minutes, stirring and making sure not to burn.
5. Add roux to sauté pan 1-teaspoon at a time while whisking to make sure roux does not lump (should have slightly thick consistency just to coat pasta).
6. Add parsley and Romano cheese and pour over 11/2 lbs. cooked penne pasta. Toss well and place in a large serving dish. Serve immediately.

SERVES 6

Portabella's   136 Broadway   Newport, RI   401.847.8200   Ed Milazzo, Chef/Owner

If you want a warm, innovative concept in Newport, Portabella is it. You never leave without meeting your friends and neighbors. It's the best Italian restaurant, deli, and market.

ED MILAZZO, CHEF/OWNER

PORTABELLA'S

In 1982 I made a deal with my mother Marie, if I got my high school diploma she would let me borrow $15,000.00, her life savings, to open up a restaurant. Looking back now I can't believe she did that, it was true blind faith! She honestly believed that I could make a restaurant succeed in a Newport storefront which was the former home of countless failed businesses.

After opening our restaurant, Puerini's, we found that we were both driven by a desire to share the wonderful food we had grown up with; we also shared something else, a naiveté about the restaurant business that could have gotten us both in serious trouble. At the time I had minimal restaurant experience, but was fortunate enough to have worked with some very talented people who taught me a great deal. Marie, on the other hand, had absolutely no experience in the restaurant business, but she jumped in headfirst. She would show up every day at lunch (at the time she had a full-time job as administrator of a national nursing service) and would help me cook, wait on tables and wash dishes.

Fettuccine Aglio e Olio with Overcooked Broccoli

8 to 10 cloves garlic
1/4 cup extra virgin olive oil
1 cup chicken or vegetable stock
1 bunch broccoli
Salt
Pepper
Crushed red pepper
Pecorino Romano cheese, grated
2 tablespoons butter
12 to 16 oz. homemade fettuccine

1. Peel garlic and slice cloves very thin.
2. Cut broccoli into pieces (about the same size as a garlic clove)
3. Put the olive oil, garlic, 1/4 teaspoon salt, 1/4 teaspoon pepper and a healthy pinch of crushed red pepper into a good-size fry pan (you will need a cover for fry pan) and cook on medium heat, stirring frequently and watching very carefully.
4. When garlic begins to brown, add 1/2 the chicken stock and cover quickly because it will splatter. When pan quiets down (about 10 seconds), add broccoli, lower heat, and cover pan. Let sit for a few minutes and then begin to add the rest of the stock a little at a time.
5. When broccoli gets mushy, take pan off heat and add butter. Let stand
6. Cook pasta...*if you can't do this without instructions, throw everything away and come to Puerini's and I'll make this dish for you!*
7. When pasta is done, strain it (don't rinse it) and add it to the broccoli sauté, toss it with the Pecorino.

Ok, now it's all done, mangia!   SERVES 4

Puerini's   24 Memorial Boulevard   Newport, RI   401.847.5506

On the weekends, our busiest time even then, she would come in and help me prep, clean, move equipment, wait on tables, take out the garbage, wash the floor and give me moral support in the face of 110 hour work weeks. After about two years of this, Marie quit her job to work full time at the restaurant.

Marie's blind faith in me was a great gamble, but I did it; however I didn't do it alone. Although there have been countless changes since then, Marie has been a constant and without her Puerini's would not exist.

PUERINI'S

Salsa

1/2 medium onion, finely diced
11/2 tablespoons fresh lime juice
6 roma tomatoes
2 jalapeno peppers, steamed, seeded and chopped
1 clove garlic
1 cup fresh cilantro, chopped
Salt to taste

1. Soak onion in lime juice for 15 minutes.
2. In a skillet roast the tomatoes, jalapenos and garlic until slightly charred. Transfer to a blender and puree for 10 seconds.
3. Combine tomato mixture in a bowl with lime juice, onion and cilantro.

MAKES 3 CUPS

Renaissance Antiques   42 Spring Street   Newport, RI   401.849.8515

Renaissance Antiques, Newport, R.I.   Muriel Barclay de Tolly 2000

Renaissance Antique Lighting is a full service lighting dealer, restorer and contractor for sales and conservation of all types of lighting dating from 1820 to 1940. We have restoration facilities to handle lighting restoration, interior and exterior, large or small.

At Renaissance Antique Lighting we can restore metal to it's original appearance without harsh machine buffing, or recreate finishes on all types of metal.

RENAISSANCE ANTIQUES

Huitres Vivarois

48 oysters (ask your fish man to open them for you)
4 oz. white wine
3 tablespoons finely chopped shallots
1 teaspoon finely chopped garlic
2 teaspoons curry powder (I prefer madras)
Juice of 1 lemon
2 cups fish stock, reduced to 4 oz. (or a 3/4 oz. bouillon cube)
2 cups heavy cream
1 teaspoon cornstarch mixed with 1 oz. water (called a slurry)
8 oz. spinach, cooked
8 oz. grated Swiss cheese

1. Preheat oven to 400°.
2. Place oysters in a covered roasting or baking pan and put in refrigerator.
3. In a saucepan combine wine, shallots, garlic, curry powder and lemon juice and bring to a boil. Add fish stock, cream and cornstarch slurry. Bring back up to a boil and season with salt and pepper. Let cool.
4. Place cooked spinach on top of oysters and finish with curry sauce. Sprinkle cheese on top and bake for about 12 minutes or until the cheese is browned.

Newport is known for it's grand mansions, luxurious yachts, and now the superb cuisine of Restaurant Bouchard. Situated in a post and beam home, the ambiance is created by Sarah Bouchard and complimented by the cuisine of her husband Albert.

Whether sitting by the fireplace, in the cozy bar, or even overlooking the action of Thames Street, you will enjoy the marvels of the ever-changing, creative, and classic French menu.

RESTAURANT BOUCHARD

STUFFED SICILIAN EGGPLANT

1 large eggplant (enough to yield 8 slices)
4 large eggs, beaten with 1/4 cup water
1 cup all-purpose flour
Canola oil for pan-frying eggplant
2 cup seasoned breadcrumbs
8 slices capicola (or your favorite ham)

8 oz. ricotta cheese
3 oz. grated Parmesan
2 cloves garlic, minced
16 slices mozzarella cheese
16 oz. favorite tomato sauce, pre-heated on
stove top
Salt and pepper to taste

1. Preheat oven to 425°.
2. Peel eggplant (if desired) and cut lengthwise into 8 equal slices. Sprinkle lightly on both sides with salt. Refrigerate for at least 20 minutes.
3. Rinse eggplant slices with water and pat dry with paper towel. Dredge each slice in flour, then egg, then seasoned breadcrumbs.
4. Heat a large sauté pan and add 1/4 cup of canola oil to start (more may be needed). Fry the eggplant slices until golden brown on both sides. Set aside on paper towel or brown bag.
5. In a large mixing bowl, mix the ricotta and grated Parmesan. Add salt and pepper to taste, as well as both cloves of minced garlic.
6. In a large (9" x 9") casserole dish place 1/2 tomato sauce.
7. When eggplant is cool enough to handle, spread each piece with ricotta mixture and add a slice of capicola and mozzarella. Roll each piece and set into casserole dish.
8. Top each bundle with a spoonful of sauce and a slice of mozzarella.
9. Bake for 8-10 minutes or until cheese starts to brown.

SERVES 4 FOR DINNER AND 8 FOR APPETIZERS

Roccos Little Italy, Newport, R.I.   Muriel Barclay de Tolly 2000

ROCCO'S LITTLE ITALY

'From Italy with Love' aptly describes the excellent cuisine and comfortable ambiance of Rocco's Little Italy, conveniently located in the heart of Newport at 124 Broadway. Rocco's Little Italy, a family tradition for over 20 years, offers superb Italian food and excellent service. A seemingly endless menu features authentic, traditional specialties of Old Italy including Veal Scallopine, Eggplant Parmigiana, lasagna, ravioli, and Chicken Cacciatore, as well as prime steaks, fresh seafood and other American selections. Every dish is cooked to order using only the freshest, finest quality ingredients. Rocco's also features a fine espresso and cappuccino bar to complement your meal.

The restaurant world is like alchemy, when you get the exact ingredients together in the right environment, and the perfect mood, you are able to create golden moments. The perfect food and wine help too, of course.

For instance, one evening a customer named Joe had planned an intimate birthday party for his wife, Mika, in our outdoor courtyard. The night was one of those thick, foggy, New England summer nights, the ground still damp from an afternoon drizzle. I had intended to move the party inside for fear of more rain, but as the evening drew near I was just able to make out a full moon showing behind gray clouds and decided that it was worth the risk.

SPICY SZECHUAN SHRIMP

My food goals are simple; stay fresh, local and, especially in the summertime, keep it light, aromatic, and fun to eat. So feel free to slurp these lemony noodles and try to keep your kitchen or dining room open and available for alchemy.

11/2 lbs. local shrimp, cleaned, rinsed and patted dry
1/8 cup canola oil
3 tablespoons toasted sesame oil
11/2 tablespoon garlic, minced
1 tablespoon fresh ginger, minced
8 tablespoons soy sauce
2 tablespoons rice wine or sake
11/2 tablespoons sugar
1 tablespoon sirachi chili sauce (any other chili sauce will do)
3/4 lb. rice noodles, cooked according (may substitute any other flat noodle)
2 carrots, peeled and cut into 1/2 inch long shreds

1 red pepper, julienned
1 yellow pepper, julienned
4 scallions, minced
1 cup cilantro or basil, picked, washed, and dried
1 lime, cut into wedges
1 cup mung bean sprouts

1. Heat a large sauté pan or wok until hot. Pour in canola oil and let get hot but not smoking. Add shrimp, stirring frequently to sear for about 3 minutes. Add garlic and ginger and let rawness cook out, about 2 minutes. Add carrots and both kinds of peppers; stir until cooked, but still crisp. Add sesame oil, all temperature to come up, then add noodles and toss all ingredients together. Add soy sauce, rice wine, chili sauce, and sugar, toss well until combined.
2. Turn out onto a platter and garnish with scallion, mung sprouts, cilantro or basil, and lime wedges.
3. Enjoy!

Salvation Cafe   140 Broadway   Newport, RI   401.847.2620

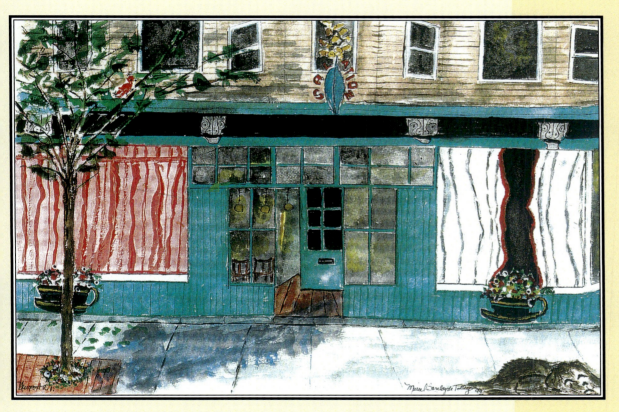

The dinner went beautifully in the candlelit garden, the mood enhanced by the sound of foghorns squeezing out their warning in the harbor. Penny, the couple's beautiful daughter had fallen asleep on a garden bench and the party was settled over the table in intimate conversation. Suddenly an incredible music came from the back gate of the garden, our eyes followed the sound to find Joe walking toward us playing his bagpipes. We were all struck with the beauty of Joe's birthday gift to Mika. It was one of those perfect golden moments.

SALVATION CAFÉ

Petti di Pollo Romano
Chicken Breast Stuffed with Mozzarella and Sautéed with Garlic, Parsley and White Wine

Four 8 oz. boneless, skinless chicken breast
12 oz. shredded mozzarella cheese
1 cup flour
1 cup dry white wine
6 sprigs parsley, chopped
8 cloves fresh garlic, finely chopped
1 stick unsalted butter

1. Pound out chicken breasts and cut in half.
2. In a bowl, mix mozzarella, garlic and parsley and roll mixture into balls about 2 inches round.
3. Place ball in center of chicken breast and secure with a toothpick, repeat for other 3 breasts.
4. In a large sauté pan heat butter. Flour chicken breasts and pat dry. When butter melts, place chicken in sauté pan and brown, turning until all sides are golden brown. Add wine and reduce.
5. Place sauté pan in a 375° oven and bake for 10 minutes, until breasts puff.
6. Serve two pieces of chicken over a bed of your favorite pasta and equally distribute sauce.

Sardella's Italian Restaurant   30 Memorial Boulevard West   Newport, RI   401.849.6312   www.sardellas.com

St George's Graduation day
Newport RII

Aniel Barclay de Tolly 2000

ST. GEORGE'S SCHOOL

St. George's School, founded in 1896, is a three hundred and twenty-five-student private school for boarding and day students in grades nine through twelve.

The breathtaking campus of St. George's, with its mixture of modern and turn of the century brick buildings, overlooks Second Beach just east of Newport, RI. Students walk to class and play sports against a scenic backdrop of wildlife preservation land and vistas of the Atlantic Ocean.

The steeple of St. George's Chapel, built in 1927-28 in the Gothic style, is the highest point of Aquidneck Island and can be seen during the day and at night for miles.

The motto of the school is 'Wisdom: the light of every life', and St. George's School offers just that in a rigorous curriculum that adheres to principles which support the healthy development of students' minds, bodies and spirits.

Harvest Vegetable Chowder

3 cups russet potato, cut into 3/4 inch pieces
2 cups sweet potato, cut into 3/4 inch pieces
11/2 cup celery, cut into 1/2 inch slices
1 cup onion, coarsely chopped
5 cups water
3 Knorr vegetable bouillon cubes
3 cups broccoli
3 cups cauliflower
3 cups carrots
10 oz. light cream
1 cup milk
1 teaspoon dried dill weed
21/2 cups cheddar cheese
Freshly ground pepper to taste

1. Combine russet and sweet potatoes, celery, onion, water and bouillon in a 4-5 quart Crock Pot slow cooker. Stir vegetables and add milk, cream and dill weed. Cover and cook about 1 hour, until the vegetables are tender.
2. Serve chowder and sprinkle with cheese and pepper.

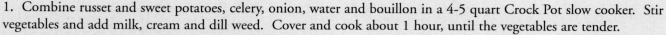

Steaming Bean Café   515 Thames Street   Newport, RI   401.849.5255

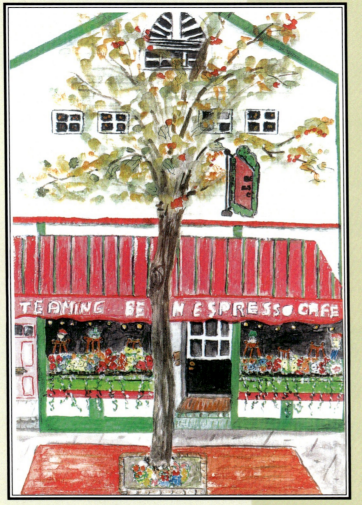

The Steaming Bean Café is a place where people and coffee of good taste get together; where the elite meet for a treat.

STEAMING BEAN CAFE

Shrimp and Feta Pasta

1/4 cup scallions
1 clove garlic
White pepper to taste
Butter for shrimp
3 or 4 jumbo shrimp, peeled and deveined
1/4 lb fettuccine
Greek feta cheese to taste
1 sprig parsley
Angel hair Parmesan cheese to taste

1. Combine butter, scallions, garlic and white pepper in a skillet and heat until butter is slightly melted. Place 3 or 4 shrimp in mixture and cook approximately three minutes on each side on medium low heat until butter burns.
2. Cook 1/4 lb fettuccine until al dente
3. Toss shrimp mixture with cooked pasta. Crumble desired amount of feta cheese on top and garnish with sprig of parsley. Serve with angel hair Parmesan cheese.

SERVES 1

The Atlantic Beach Club   53 Purgatory Road   Middletown, RI   401.847.2750

Formerly known as Johnny's House of Seafood, The Atlantic Beach Club has the distinction of being the only restaurant on Aquidneck Island located RIGHT ON THE BEACH.

Our restaurant has become a tradition in Newport and is widely known for our fabulous menu, which features seafood and traditional dishes prepared with pride. Our Johnny's Clamcakes and fried clams are known worldwide and are a must while you are in Newport.

In the summer, our vast patio bar welcomes you to bask in the sun while enjoying the sounds of New England's hottest bands and the most amazing view of the Atlantic Ocean and Newport's famous Cliff Walk.

We look forward to having you as our guest! Enjoy! Bon Appetit! Kale Orexi!

THE ATLANTIC BEACH CLUB

In the latter part of the 1800's, Richard Canfield, still restless despite great profit at his New York and Saratoga clubs, decided to take over the Nautilus Club in Newport. It gave him another whack at the wealthy after the racing season ended. He purchased the Newport property for $65,000 in 1897 from Ferdinand Abell who had a controlling interest in the Brooklyn National League baseball team. Canfield's profits of eight years in Newport were $500,000, but business dwindled near the end. The profit in the 1904 season amounted to a mere $1,100. Reggie Vanderbilt and some friends appeared the day after the house was closed and begged for one spin of the roulette wheel. Vanderbilt put $1,000 on the red and won which left Canfield with a $100 profit for the year. The house was sold in 1905 to Dave Bucklin and Billy Coe who had been associated with Canfield in other ventures.

SAM WILLIAMSON'S CANFIELD HOUSE SCALLOPS

4 oranges
1/4 cup Grand Marnier
1/2 stick unsalted butter, cubed
1/4 cup Grenadine
30 large scallops
Vegetable oil

1. Zest oranges. Place zest in bowl and cover with Grenadine, set aside. After zest has colored, place on paper towel to dry.
2. Cut oranges in 1/2 and squeeze juice into saucepan, adding rinds. Add Grand Marnier and reduce until thick.
3. Strain and remove rinds, return sauce to heat and whip butter cubes in slowly. Season to taste with salt and pepper.
4. Heat skillet with vegetable oil. Salt and pepper scallops before pan searing. Be sure not to overcook.
5. To plate, place warm orange sauce on plate, placing scallops on top of sauce. Garnish with ruby red colored orange zest.

Summer vegetables are suggested as an accompaniment.

SERVES 6

The Canfield House   5 Memorial Boulevard   Newport, RI   401.847.0416

Canfield casinos have been compared with Monte Carlo because of the high play in them. Ordinary limits of play at roulette tables were in some cases double those at Monte Carlo. Canfield allowed men known to be capable of standing a heavy loss to double and even quadruple the ordinary limit. Nearly $500,000 in cash was kept in the Newport house to pay off winners. Canfield used much of his profit to furnish the Newport house with antiques and other objects of art. He insisted on comfort and elegant surroundings for his patrons.

THE CANFIELD HOUSE

MINESTRONE DI FAGIOLI DI MONTERIGGIONE BEAN SOUP FROM MONTERIGGIONE

1 lb. kale, cleaned and stalks removed
1 lb. Savoy cabbage
4 medium carrots
2 large celery stalks
2 large red onions
10 sprigs Italian parsley, leaves only
5 large fresh basil leaves

1/4 lb. pancetta, cut fine
1/2 cup olive oil
3 cans cannellini beans and liquid (Pastene brand recommended)
1 lb. can Italian tomatoes and liquid, cut coarsely
Salt and pepper to taste
1 sprig fresh tarragon
Eight 5-inch slices Tuscan bread, 3 inches thick (optional)

1. Cut the kale and cabbage in thin strips and soak in cold water for 15 minutes.
2. Finely chop carrots, celery, onions, parsley, and basil.
3. Sauté chopped pancetta and olive oil for 5 minutes in a stockpot. Add chopped vegetables and basil and sauté for 2 minutes more.
4. Drain the kale and cabbage and add to the pot, cook for 10 minutes.
5. Add the cannellini beans and liquid to pot, and then add canned tomatoes and juice to pot. Cook covered and simmer for 1 hour.
6. Add salt, pepper, and tarragon.
7. Using a food mill and medium disk coarsely purée soup.
8. Place one Tuscan bread slice on the bottom of each bowl and pour soup over it to serve. (Soup should have a thick consistency).

SERVES 8

The Golden Pear   69 Mill St.   Newport, RI   401.846.6582

If you want to experience the feeling of Tuscany and Provence, you simply must visit the Golden Pear. In our tran-quil setting you'll find European-style furniture designed by our master crafts-men, luxurious imported fabrics to enhance any room décor, colorful Italian majolica and many unusual decorative accents to help you in creating 'la belle vita'.

Located at the corner of Mill and Spring Streets, we have private parking for your conve-nience.

THE GOLDEN PEAR

Come spend some time at The John Easton House and experience a delightful mixture of elegance, charm, and warm hospitality. Celebrating her fourth year as the B&B's proprietor, Jan Taylor creates an atmosphere where the guests feel pampered, restful and excited to explore the many sites of Newport. Whether you are snacking on the complimentary homemade brownies, or just sitting outside relaxing on the comfortable front lawn, you will know you made the right choice by visiting The John Easton House.

Jan prepares a full breakfast in which everyone's appetites are taken into consideration. If you love a traditional country breakfast, including freshly baked breads and muffins, or if you prefer a lighter fare of yogurt, fresh fruit, and cereal, you will find it at The John Easton House.

The B&B offers five air-conditioned rooms, all with private baths, in a non-smoking environment, with fireplaces and suites available. Room rates are very reasonable, ranging from $140.00 to $165.00 per night for double occupancy.

'TO DIE FOR' FRENCH TOAST

1 cup brown sugar
1/2 cup butter
2 tablespoons corn syrup
5 medium tart apples, peeled and sliced

5 eggs
11/2 cup milk
1 teaspoon vanilla
1 loaf French bread

1. Cook sugar, butter, and syrup until syrupy and pour into a sprayed 9x13-inch baking dish.
2. Spread apple slices over syrup mixture.
3. Slice bread into 3/4 inch slices and place on top of apple slices.
4. Whisk together remaining ingredients and pour over bread. Cover and refrigerate overnight.
5. Bake uncovered for 40 minutes in a 350° oven. Serve with SPICY APPLE SYRUP (recipe follows).

SPICY APPLE SYRUP

1 cup applesauce
One 10 oz. jar apple jelly
1/2 teaspoon cinnamon
1/8 teaspoon ground cloves
Dash salt

Combine all ingredients in small saucepan. Cook over medium heat, stirring constantly until jelly melts and syrup is hot.

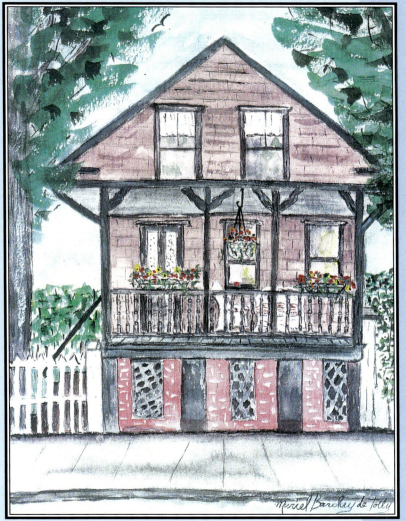

We purchased our home, located in "The Point" section of Newport, in 1987 and are only the third owners since it was built in 1898. The Point is the oldest section of Newport where some of the country's history was shaped and traditions have always been cherished.

The Point Association's forty-five years have been marked by many accomplishments and positive changes, showing how determined and dedicated people can effect what happens in their community. For example, numerous houses have been and are being restored, some of which antedate the Revolution, and many trees and shrubs have been planted. In addition, Battery and John Martin Parks were created and beautified with trees and memorial benches, and Storer Park was purchased, landscaped, and deeded to the City. How fortunate we are to live in this friendly, caring community by the sea!

"THE POINT"

Runcible Spoon's Buttermilk Pancakes

From a recipe handed down to Joan from her Grandmother Mikolite

3 cups buttermilk
3 eggs
11/2 teaspoon baking soda
11/2 teaspoon salt
2 cups flour
1/2 cup plus 1 tablespoon vegetable oil

Preparation
1. Combine eggs and buttermilk.
2. Add baking soda and salt to the liquid mixture and stir in flour.
3. Add in oil and stir. It's okay to have some small lumps in the final batter.

Cooking (Our experience is based on using an electric griddle at about 400°)
1. Pour 1/4 to 1/3 cup batter onto griddle for each pancake.
2. Flip after bottom begins to brown.
3. Cook until done, test one or two to determine your particular cooking time.

Serving Suggestions
We enjoy our pancakes with pure maple syrup, and depending on what's available in the garden or fresh in the market, we like to add fruit to our cakes. So, experiment with this wonderful and easy recipe...maybe add berries to the mixture before you cook them, or nuts afterward. Grated coconut sounds interesting too. Enjoy!

SERVES 4-6

Walk through the front door of the Victorian Ladies Inn and know that you are welcomed. The Inn has been restored and decorated elegantly but with comfort in mind. Each guestroom has its own personality, with period pieces and lots of wonderful fabrics. The property has lovely gardens and courtyards, complete with a Koi-filled fishpond. Convenient to downtown Newport, the Inn is within walking distance to the beaches, the Cliff Walk, as well as many of Newport's other sites of interest. A full, gourmet breakfast is served daily.

THE VICTORIAN LADIES INN

Tropical Turkey Melt

1 English muffin, split
1 teaspoon Dijon mustard
3 oz. smoked turkey slices
3 thin slices papaya
1 slice Monterey Jack cheese
Butter or margarine, softened

1. Spread inside muffin halves with mustard. On one half, layer turkey, papaya and cheese. Press remaining muffin half, mustard side down, over cheese.
2. Spread butter on outsides of muffin halves.
3. Cook sandwich in small skillet over medium heat until toasted, about 4 minutes. Flip and cook on remaining side until toasted and cheese is melted. Serve hot.

SERVES 1

The Weatherly Cottage   30 Weatherly Avenue   Newport, RI   401.849.8371

This lovely, traditional cottage has been operating for ten years and is located in the quiet, southern end of Newport. Close by are some tennis courts and a number of Newport attractions, including the mansions; the area is rather scenic and great for walking. Your hostess, Patti, will help you plan your day and tell you in detail about the various sights to be seen.

There are two guest rooms at the Cottage; one offers a private entrance and private bath with a refrigerator, television, air conditioning, telephone and small sitting area. The other guest room is a lovely area on the other side of the Cottage, which features a charming four-poster bed. For guests who would like to relax we have a handsome family room looking onto a pleasant deck and attractive gardens for your use. The Cottage serves a full breakfast and afternoon snacks are available.

The Weatherly Cottage has reasonable rates with mid-week specials, and is open April through October. The establishment is registered and belongs to NIBBs and the Newport County Bed and Breakfast Association. Parking is no problem at all. Try us; you'll like the Cottage.

THE WEATHERLY COTTAGE
BED AND BREAKFAST

80

CARDAMOM-SCENTED RACK OF LAMB

2 eight bone lamb racks, frenched
2 tablespoons toasted and ground cardamom seed
2 tablespoons olive oil

1 medium-sized beet, peeled and diced
2 carrots, peeled and diced
2 parsnips, peeled and diced
2 sprigs fresh thyme
2 sprigs fresh rosemary
1/2 oz. olive oil
Salt and pepper to taste

4 cups Swiss chard, cleaned and stemmed
1 tablespoon minced garlic
1 oz. olive oil
Salt and pepper to taste

2 medium-sized sweet potatoes, peeled and diced
2 tablespoons butter
1 tablespoon toasted and ground cardamom
2 tablespoons maple syrup
Salt and white pepper to taste

2 cups red wine
2 cups veal stock
4 tablespoons Maille mustard
2 tablespoons chopped garlic
2 tablespoons chopped shallots
2 tablespoons tomato paste
4 sprigs fresh thyme
1 tablespoon black peppercorn

FOR THE LAMB:
Rinse and pat dry. Rub the lamb with cardamom and place in a hot sauté pan and sear until a crisp crust forms. Remove from sauté pan and roast in a 350° oven until desired doneness. (10-12 min. for medium rare)

WHOLE GRAIN MUSTARD BORDELAISE SAUCE:
Sweat down the shallots, garlic, thyme, black peppercorns and tomato paste for 2 minutes. Deglaze with the red wine and allow to reduce by 1/2. Add in the veal stock and reduce by 1/2, strain through fine sieve and whisk in mustard. Reserve.

FOR THE SWEET POTATOES:
Boil until fork tender. Strain and place in a mixing bowl. On medium speed slowly mix in maple syrup, butter and cardamom until well incorporated.

FOR THE VEGETABLES:
Toss all ingredients in a large bowl and mix well. Place in a roasting pan and cook in a 350° oven for 12-15 minutes. Remove from oven and reserve.

TO PLATE:
Quickly wilt the Swiss chard. Ladle the sauce in the middle of the plate. Place Swiss chard in middle of plate and spoon on the sweet potatoes and roasted vegetables. Split the racks into 2-4 bone portions and place on top of vegetables and sweet potato. Garnish with fresh rosemary sprig.

For well over three hundred years, people have been gathering at the White Horse Tavern to relax in front of one of our many fireplaces, enjoy a bit of food and perhaps a drink or two.

Today the White Horse Tavern is Rhode Island's flagship restaurant. Customers can experience truly elegant dining and gracious service in the same colonial setting where our forefathers helped to shape the course of the nation. We specialize in sophisticated American cuisine using fresh, local ingredients. Our award-winning wine list offers over three hundred selections from around the world.

In addition to our public dining, private rooms are available which can accommodate groups from four to fifty persons. The historic White Horse Tavern is the perfect place to celebrate special occasions, entertain business associates or host a wedding rehearsal dinner. Jackets are required. Reservations are suggested.

THE WHITE HORSE TAVERN

KOULOURAKIA Greek Sesame seed Cookies

1 cup sweet butter
11/2 cups sugar
1 teaspoon vanilla extract
3 eggs
5 cups self-rising flour
1/2 teaspoon ground cinnamon
1/2 cup sesame seeds
1 egg yolk, beaten

1. Cream butter until light and fluffy. Add sugar and vanilla extract and beat well. Add eggs 1 at a time and beat well after each addition. Add cinnamon.
2. Sift flour and add to creamed mixture to form soft dough. Chill for several hours or overnight.
3. To form cookies, use a tablespoon of dough and roll into a 3.5-inch rope. Form into a braid shape, like a figure eight, pinching at the end. Place several inches apart on a greased baking sheet. Brush tops of cookies with egg yolk and sprinkle with sesame seeds.
4. Bake at 375° for 15 minutes or until lightly browned. Cool on a rack and store in an airtight container.

MAKES 6-DOZEN COOKIES

Edward and Tracie Kedzierski   Top of the Hill   Newport,RI

We were first attracted to our gracious, turn of the century Victorian house for its truly unique wrap-around porch...ideal for summer entertaining. What a wonderful world we see from our porch while either enjoying our morning coffee or relaxing in the early evenings with a glass of wine. We truly see a magnificent world in our lovely Greenough Place location.

TOP OF THE HILL

Panzanella Salad

1/4 cup capers
1 large cucumber, decoratively peeled and sliced
1/2 red onion
4 plum tomatoes, diced
1 large red pepper, cut into 1-inch cubes
1 large yellow pepper, cut into 1-inch cubes

1/2 cup Kalamata olives
1/2 loaf French or Italian bread, cut into 11/2-inch cubes
1/2 cup fresh basil leaves, chiffonade
1 cup water
Kosher salt and coarse ground pepper to taste
Basil leaves and flowers for garnish

1. Moisten cubed bread by soaking in water and squeezing out excess.
2. Prepare vegetables and toss together with bread in a large bowl.

FOR DRESSING:

Approx. 3/4 cup balsamic vinegar
Approx. 1/4 cup extra virgin olive oil

1. Pour balsamic vinegar in a small bowl and, while briskly whisking, slowly drizzle olive oil into vinegar. 2. When dressing is completely combined and slightly emulsified, toss with vegetables and bread. Add salt and pepper and transfer into a large salad bowl, garnish and buon apetito!

SERVES 4

Trattoria Simpatico, established in May of 1993, is situated on the picturesque island of Jamestown. Owner Phyllis Bedard founded the restaurant with the philosophy of pleasing her customers and creating the best dining atmosphere possible.

Dining is offered not only in the charming house, but also in a tastefully decorated awning area and the 'al fresco' bar and patio. During the summer, you can hear live jazz five nights a week and in the winter on Thursday evenings.

Over the years her chefs have experimented with Italian, Mediterranean, and Asian cuisine, but one of the most popular and savored dishes is from her original menu in 1993 (and it keeps making a comeback every summer), the Panzanella or 'Tuscan Bread' salad.

TRATTORIA SIMPATICO

When you walk into Tucker's Bistro you feel that you have stepped back in time. The deep red lacquered walls filled with paintings by local artists, large chandeliers made with chicken wire, and the voices of singers such as Edith Piaf, Ella Fitzgerald, Marlene Dietrich, and Louis Armstrong make you think, 'Am I on Broadway in Newport, or in some Paris Bistro in the 1920's?'

Co-owners Tucker Harris and Ellen Retlev are in their fifth year of operation. They have designed it so that each table is set eclectically with different china, silverware and small lamps on each table, giving you the feeling that the table has been set just for you; well-worn rugs and dim lighting complete the atmosphere.

The menu is fusion and is not limited to any style or country. If you would like to take your shoes off and enjoy some comfort food, Shepard's Pie and Beef Bourguignon is offered during the cold nights of the winter months. Other seafood dishes are available, for instance, fresh Grilled Native Scallops served over a lobster-mango cream sauce and Seafood Creole made with an array of seafood in a New Orleans-style Creole sauce.

BANANA BREAD PUDDING

11/2 loaves of day-old French bread, sliced
12 very ripe bananas, sliced
3 eggs
3/4 cup brown sugar
1/4 cup Myers rum
1 quart heavy cream

1. Mix together eggs, brown sugar, rum and cream to make custard.
2. Layer in a large pan 1/3 the sliced French bread, 6 bananas (sliced) and 1/2 custard mixture, repeat process for second layer using the rest of the custard and bananas. Top with the last 1/3 sliced bread and press to moisten top layer.
3. Cook covered for 1 hour 15 minutes at 350°.
4. Uncover and cook for 15 minutes more, or until golden brown.

CRÈME ANGLAISE

3 egg yolks
1/2 cup sugar
1/2 cup milk
1/2 cup heavy cream
1/4 cup Myers rum

1. In a double boiler, cook egg yolks and sugar until thickened, add warm milk and heavy cream. Add rum last.
Serve the bread pudding warm and top with crème Anglaise.
OPTION: Instead of making crème Anglaise, melt vanilla ice cream and add a little rum.

Tucker's Bistro   150 Broadway   Newport, RI   401.846.3449

Newport, R.I.

Muriel Barclay de Tolly 2000

The Shrimp Sambal with a Malaysian curry sauce and the Tenderloin of Pork served with a ginger, soy and garlic glaze give the menu an Asian influence. Tucker's appetizers and salads also offer a bevy of wonderful surprises, such as the Escargot in a sun-dried tomato beurre blanc, Grilled Portabella mushrooms, Crab Cakes with a remoulade sauce and a house favorite, Pear Salad served over mesclun greens with sliced pears, spicy walnuts and gorgonzola cheese with a cranberry vinaigrette. Daily specials are also offered, a favorite find is fresh striped bass caught by local fishermen and prepared many ways by our chef.

With the incredible atmosphere, wonderful menu and the selection of wine or cocktails, we are sure that you will have a romantic evening for two or a great time with a group of your friends.

TUCKER'S BISTRO

BLACK OLIVE PÂTÉ

In Italy, this pâté is served with a quarter-inch layer of extra virgin olive oil over the top, which tends to be a little too messy and filling. I also discovered that canned olives taste better than the more expensive deli varieties; they have much less salt and let the wonderful, nutty flavors of the roasted garlic and toasted pignoli nuts play against the spiciness of the oregano and saltiness of the parmesan cheese. This pâté can be made ahead of time and refrigerated for several days, making it more flavorful.

3 cups canned, pitted, and drained black olives
1/2 cup extra virgin olive oil
4 large cloves roasted garlic
1/4 cup lightly toasted pignoli nuts or almonds
1/4 teaspoon garlic powder
1/4 cup grated Parmesan cheese
3 tablespoons dried, crushed oregano
1/4 teaspoon salt
1/4 cup finely diced sweet red peppers
1/4 cup yellow and red tomatoes

1. In a food processor with the knife blade mix olives, olive oil, roasted garlic, and pignoli nuts to a coarse or chunky consistency
2. Evenly sprinkle garlic powder, Parmesan cheese, oregano, and salt over mixture and process to a granular consistency (this pâté is not meant to be smooth!).
3. Place mixture in a two-cup serving dish and garnish with a mixture of cold peppers and tomatoes around the rim of the dish. Finish off with a sprinkle of Parmesan cheese on the top.
4. Serve room temperature with plain-flavored crackers or crusty Italian bread.

Twin Peaks   Amy and Michael Barclay de Tolly   Jamestown, RI

My husband and I started our married life in Jamestown soon after honeymooning in beautiful southern Italy. This recipe comes from the delightful restaurants we enjoyed in Sienna and Florence. Soon after sitting down for dinner, the waiter would bring this wonderful appetizer with fresh bread to the table. We deciphered the main ingredients, although I have made a few small adjustments. Without a doubt, this recipe remains a favorite of mine since it is a quick, slick and delicious appetizer for any occasion.

TWIN PEAKS

Wapping Roadside Blueberry Kuchen

1 cup + 2 tablespoons flour, divided
1/8 teaspoon salt
1/8 teaspoon cinnamon
1/2 cup butter or margarine, softened
2 tablespoons + 2/3 cup sugar, divided
5 cups blueberries, divided

Preheat oven to 400°. In bowl, mix 1 cup flour, salt, and 2 tablespoons sugar. Cut in butter and shape into dough and with lightly floured fingers, press into bottom and sides of 9-inch layer cake pan. Add blueberries and bake on lowest rack for 50-60 minutes or until crust is well-browned and filling bubbles. Cool after baking.

8 SERVINGS

Wapping Roadside Stand   902 Wapping Road   Portsmouth, RI

PORTSMOUTH, R.I.

Maricel Bardby-de Tolly 99

Take a drive in the country. Breathe the fresh air and enjoy the good life with our homemade breads and baked good, berries in season, and cold drinks.

Off the beaten path, Wapping Roadside Stand is one of the only places where you will find rare varieties of flowers and herbs, heirloom plants and hanging baskets. Container plant design and window box planting services are our specialty.

From Newport:
Head north on Rte. 138 (East Main Road) until you reach the third stop light at the intersection of Sandy Point Road and East Main Road. Turn right onto Sandy Point Road. Take your first right onto Wapping Road. The stand is on your left.

WAPPING ROADSIDE STAND

LAMB LOIN IN PECAN CRUST WITH SWEET POTATO HAY

BALSAMIC SAUCE

1/2 cup balsamic vinegar
1 teaspoon shallots or onions
Salt and pepper to taste
1/2 heavy cream
2 tablespoons butter
Salt and pepper to taste

1. Sauté shallots lightly, until translucent.
2. Add balsamic vinegar and reduce to a third.
3. Add cream and reduce by half. Slowly add the butter in little pieces while whisking or stirring the sauce, season with a little salt and pepper and keep warm until ready to serve.

LAMB

2 6oz. boneless lamb loins
1/2 cup flour
2 eggs lightly beaten with 1 tablespoon milk
1/4 cup breadcrumbs
1/2 cup pecans - chopped very fine

1. Combine breadcrumbs and pecans thoroughly.
2. Dredge lamb in flour then dip in egg batter and roll in pecan/bread crumb mixture, making sure you get a heavy coating of crumbs. This step can be done six hours ahead of time.
3. Lightly sauté lamb in olive oil until golden brown on all sides. Finish in the oven for 5 minutes at 400° for medium rare or longer for desired temperature.

SWEET POTATO HAY

1 peeled sweet potato - julienned fine
1/4 cup olive oil

1. Heat olive oil and add sweet potatoes, fry until golden brown.

Yesterdays and "The Place"   28 Washington Square   Newport, RI   401.847.0116

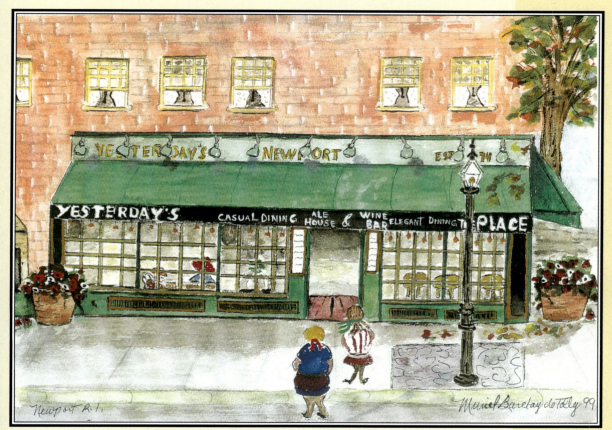

A unique dining experience which offers two entirely different restaurants under one roof. 'Yesterdays Ale House' is in it's 25th year under the same ownership and features a turn of the century atmosphere with a menu designed for the whole family, including award winning entrees, salads, grilled pizza, black angus burger, vegetarian selections, nachos and more.

'The Place' is the insider's best-kept secret in Newport, offering intimate dining with the most cutting edge cuisine. Wine Enthusiast Magazine said 'it is one of the eight must eat at restaurants.' This is truly a restaurant not to be missed. Limited seating.

YESTERDAYS AND "THE PLACE"

94

Last but not least, this delightful French bakery was my first attempt at painting a building. I am so happy I found this creative outlet at this time in my life. Painting does warm the soul.

Muriel Barclay de Tolly

BOULANGERIE OBELIX

Boulangerie Obelix   Spring Street   Newport, RI